Butterflies

by Susan Jones Leeming

PEARSON
Scott Foresman

Editorial Offices: Glenview, Illinois • Parsippany, New Jersey • New York, New York
Sales Offices: Needham, Massachusetts • Duluth, Georgia • Glenview, Illinois
Coppell, Texas • Ontario, California • Mesa, Arizona

Every effort has been made to secure permission and provide appropriate credit for photographic material. The publisher deeply regrets any omission and pledges to correct errors called to its attention in subsequent editions.

Unless otherwise acknowledged, all photographs are the property of Scott Foresman, a division of Pearson Education.

Photo locators denoted as follows: Top (T), Center (C), Bottom (B), Left (L), Right (R), Background (Bkgd)

Opener: Peter Arnold, Inc.; 1 Aurora & Quanta Productions Inc.; 3 Brand X Pictures; 4 Brand X Pictures; 5 Brand X Pictures; 6 Brand X Pictures; 7 Aurora & Quanta Productions Inc.; 8 Peter Arnold, Inc.; 9 Brand X Pictures; 10 Brand X Pictures; 12 Brand X Pictures; 13 Brand X Pictures; 15 Brand X Pictures;

ISBN: 0-328-13192-X

9 10 V010 14 13 12 11 10 09 08

Have you ever seen a butterfly flutter by? Have you looked at its colorful wings? Have you watched it land on flowers? Read on to learn about this amazing **insect.**

A butterfly does not begin its life **cycle** as a butterfly. First, there's an egg. When the egg hatches, a caterpillar comes out. The caterpillar eats and eats and eats. Soon it grows large.

Caterpillar

Egg

When the caterpillar's big enough, it hangs from a branch. Then it changes into a chrysalis. The chrysalis will **develop** into a butterfly.

Chrysalis

After about two weeks, the waiting is done. The chrysalis has developed into a butterfly. The butterfly pushes out of its old skin. It shivers because its wings are wet. It rests in the sun and waits for its wings to dry.

A butterfly comes out of the chrysalis.

Once its wings are dry, the butterfly flies off to find food. Many butterflies eat **nectar,** the sweet juice made by flowers. With its long tongue, a butterfly can suck nectar out of the middle of flowers.

Like all insects, the butterfly has two **antennae,** or feelers, on its head. These help the butterfly know what's around it. The butterfly also has feet that help it crawl on flowers. The feet help the butterfly taste too. A butterfly lands on a flower and knows how it tastes!

A butterfly visits many flowers each day. During the night and on rainy days, the butterfly rests. The butterfly finds a dry branch or leaf to use as a resting place. It may rest there for many hours.

This butterfly visits flowers.

Have you seen the many colors on the wings of a butterfly? The colors make the butterfly beautiful. But beauty is not the only reason the colors are there. The colors help the butterfly. Do you know how? They're **camouflage.** They help the butterfly hide from danger.

Camouflage makes this butterfly hard to see.

Butterflies are in danger from other insects or animals that want to eat them. Birds and other **predators** try to catch and eat butterflies. Butterflies use their camouflage colors to hide.

The bright colors of other butterflies warn enemies that they don't taste good. They may even be **poisonous** or dangerous to eat. These brightly colored butterflies are safe because birds and other insects know they taste bad.

If their colors aren't enough to **protect** them, butterflies use their wings to fly away. Some butterflies can fly faster than people can run. Once butterflies are safe, they come back to the flowers. There they eat, lay eggs, and begin the life cycle all over again.

Now Try This

Watching Butterflies Grow

You and your classmates can watch butterflies develop. See them change from caterpillars to chrysalises to beautiful butterflies ready for flight.

You'll need

- a box, large jar, or a terrarium
- a cloth or mesh screen
- branches, dirt, and leaves that your caterpillar likes to eat

Here's How to Do It!

1. Find or order caterpillars. If it is the spring or fall, you may be able to find caterpillars on trees or grass near your school. If not, you can order caterpillars on the Internet or from a nature store. Ask an adult for help.

2. Identify the caterpillars. Using a butterfly identification book, match your caterpillars with the ones in the book. Then put them in the home you made for them.

3. Watch for chrysalises to form. Wait for butterflies to emerge. When the butterflies hatch, place fresh flowers and fruit slices into the butterfly box to feed them. On a warm day, release your butterflies into the wild. Watch as they fly away!

Glossary

antennae *n.* long, thin feelers on the heads of insects.

camouflage *n.* a shape or color that makes a living thing hard to see.

cycle *n.* something that repeats or moves in the same order over and over again.

develop *v.* to grow.

insect *n.* an animal without bones and with a body in three parts.

nectar *n.* sweet liquid in many flowers.

poisonous *adj.* containing poison.

predators *n.* animals that eat other animals.

protect *v.* to keep safe.